Papercrafts for
Children

Papercrafts for Children

18 fun projects using paper, paints and stamps

Vivienne Bolton

NH
NEW
HOLLAND

For my grandparents, Scotty and Ella Waters

Thanks to publishing manager Rosemary Wilkinson, editor Corinne Masciocchi
and photographer Shona Wood for all their hard work and enthusiasm for this project.

First published in 2006 by New Holland Publishers (UK) Ltd
London • Cape Town • Sydney • Auckland

Garfield House
86–88 Edgware Road
London W2 2EA
United Kingdom
www.newhollandpublishers.com

80 McKenzie Street
Cape Town 8001
South Africa

Level 1, Unit 4
14 Aquatic Drive
Frenchs Forest
NSW 2086
Australia

218 Lake Road
Northcote
Auckland
New Zealand

ISBN 1 84537 247 6

Senior Editor: Corinne Masciocchi
Designer: Gülen Shevki-Taylor
Photographer: Shona Wood
Production: Hazel Kirkman
Editorial Direction: Rosemary Wilkinson

10 9 8 7 6 5 4 3 2 1

Reproduction by Modern Age, Hong Kong
Printed and bound by Times Offset, Malaysia

Contents

Introduction

My happiest childhood memories are of playing in my grandparents' home. Creativity was always encouraged, and I was incredibly fortunate to grow up with an extended family of very imaginative people. I would make books from scraps of paper, mould soft soap into dolly baths for my doll's house or draw paper dolls on a tray, sat at one end of the table while my grandmother sewed wedding dresses for a living at the other end. With the encouragement of my grandparents, I spent many happy hours turning shoe boxes into doll's houses. I moulded doll's house food from plasticine and my grandmother would watch over me as I stood at the stove cooking up clay or placing trays of salt and flour dough models in the oven to bake. I made fairy rings in the garden decorated with charms, flowers and leaves, and spent hours fiddling around in my grandfather's workshop hammering bits of driftwood and left-over bits and pieces into boats, cars or miniature furniture.

When my children were growing up, I kept a 'useful box' full of suitable craft equipment and materials specifically for them to craft with. They loved it, and as long as I managed to keep the 'useful box' well stocked *my* craft materials were safe! This useful box contained left-over sheets of Christmas gift wrap, small boxes, plastic bottle tops (they make great wheels!), paints, felt-tip pens, crayons and pencils. When out shopping, I would purchase discounted craft materials, glitters and other odds and ends I thought might come in handy. Whenever I completed a 'work' project, the left-over bits and pieces would go into the 'useful box', too. I still save things, but now the bits and pieces get sent to my niece Scarlett.

I hope you and your children enjoy the projects laid out in this book, but please encourage your children to use the ideas and techniques to create new designs. The best you can do for your children is to inspire them, encourage their endeavours and anything is possible! Success will build confidence, and confidence is one of the building blocks of a happy and successful life.

I wish you many happy hours crafting with your children!

Vivienne Bolton

Materials and equipment

BASIC EQUIPMENT

1. Coloured papers come in packs or pads. These are great for children and economical to buy.

2. Funky Foam this brilliant craft material can be cut out and decorated with 3-D paint and stuck together with glue, tape or staples.

3. Handmade paper has an interesting texture but as the colours are natural, they tend to fade in sunlight.

4. Crêpe paper has a crinkle finish and can be stretched slightly into shapes. Use staples or glue to attach one piece to another, as most sticky tapes do not adhere well due to its crinkly surface.

5. Tissue paper very fine paper that can be stamped or stencilled into home-made gift wrap.

6. Scissors invest in a good pair of children's sturdy safety scissors. NEVER allow children to use craft knives.

7. PVA glue (craft glue) is a good all-round glue to keep in your craft box.

8. Glue stick remember to replace the lid to make sure the glue doesn't dry out!

9. Stapler make sure you purchase one that uses standard staples.

10. Masking tape comes in a variety of widths and is great for holding card together.

11. Double-sided tape comes in various widths. It's often easier to use than glue as it is less messy.

GLITTERS, PAINTS AND STICKY STUFF

1. 3-D paint should be used under supervision. It comes in a variety of colours and can be used to decorate fabric, Funky Foam, paper and card.

2. Glitter glue comes in lots of colours including clear, gold and silver. You can often use glitter glue instead of loose glitter as it is less messy. It takes a while to dry so be careful not to smudge it!

3. Terrifically Tacky Tape is a special high-stick tape to which beads and thread will firmly attach. A heat source is required to set the glue on this tape.

4. Micro beads produce great effects but are not suitable for children to use without adult supervision as they are very small and get everywhere.

5. Gems and stickers gems can be used to decorate projects and should be stuck down with PVA glue or double-sided tape. Stickers come in all sorts of shapes, sizes and colours and can be purchased from most craft shops. They make quick and easy decorations on cards and almost any craft project.

6. Paintbrush a selection of paintbrushes always comes in useful. Good quality ones are worth the extra expense. Make sure you rinse them thoroughly when you have finished with them.

7. Braid and lace come in all sorts of designs and colourways. They can be attached with glue or double-sided tape.

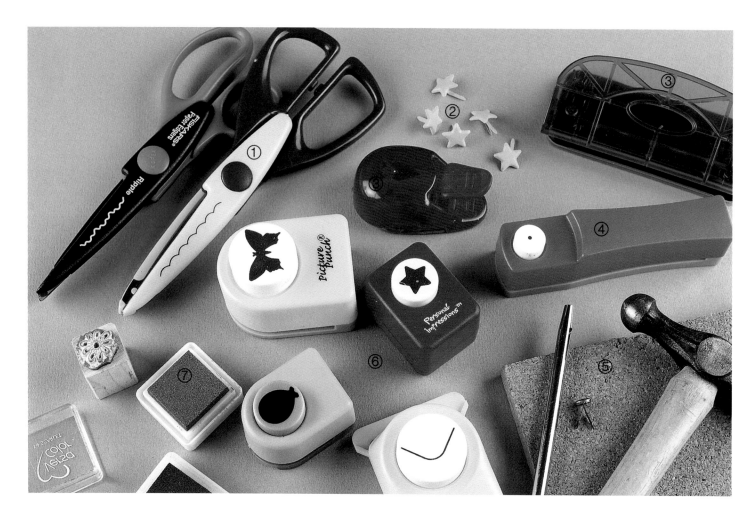

STAMPS, PUNCHES AND FASTENERS

1. Decorative-edge scissors come with all sorts of pretty edges and can cut through Funky Foam as easily as paper.

2. Paper fasteners traditionally, paper fasteners were small, round, brass button shapes with two arms that opened out through a hole made in the paper. Nowadays, you can purchase paper fasteners in almost every shape and colour.

3. Hole punches make single or double holes in paper, card and Funky Foam.

4. Craft punch makes pin-size holes in card or paper.

5. Hole punch, hammer and mat hole punches come in a selection of shapes: simple round holes or a flower or heart. You will need a mat to hammer onto so your work surface is not spoiled.

6. Decorative punches are great fun. A selection of these comes in very useful for almost any craft project. Butterfly, flower and balloon punches are just some of the punches used in this book.

7. Stamps and stamp pad stamps are great for decorating paper to use as gift wrap and making doll's house wallpaper. Children can make their own stamps made from Funky Foam (see p 23). Stamp pads come in a variety of colours and sizes. Make sure children replace lids after use as stamp pads dry up fast!

SHOP-BOUGHT AND HOME-MADE CLAYS

1. Play clay (also known as plasticine) is made from waxes and oils, which means it does not harden and can be remodelled as many times as you like. Play clay is readily available but you can make something similar yourself (see below).

2. Polymer clay is suitable for use by children aged 8 years and over. An adult is required to bake finished items in a kitchen oven. Good for making wheels, model animals, brooches and doll's house furniture.

3. Air-drying clay is very useful and great fun! It is found in toy and craft shops, comes in many colours and is easy to use. You can, of course, make your own at home (see below).

Home-made play clay

1 cup flour
½ cup salt
2 tsp cream of tartar
1 cup water
Food colouring (as much as you need to achieve the required colour)
1 Tbsp cooking oil

Place all the ingredients in a saucepan over a medium heat and stir well with a wooden spoon until the mixture forms a ball. Remove from the heat and turn out onto a clean work surface. Allow to cool then knead well. Store in an airtight container.

Home-made air-drying clay

4 slices of white bread, crusts removed
Powder paint, to colour
2 Tbsp PVA glue (craft glue)
4 drops glycerine (from the chemist)

Use fingertips or a blender to crumb the bread. Place the breadcrumbs, powder paint and glue in a small throw-away container. Use a lolly stick to mix the ingredients together until a ball is formed. Rub glycerine on your fingers so that the dough does not stick to them, and knead the dough until it is smooth.

Wrap the dough in plastic film and place in a plastic bag to avoid it drying out. Leave modelled items in a warm, dry place to harden.

Decorated pencils

Ladybird, ladybird, fly away home! Can you see the ladybirds on the Funky Foam leaves? I found these coloured pencils in a discount store and used 3-D paint to turn them into mini masterpieces. I chose a flowery design and made leaves from Funky Foam. You might want to paint on the ladybirds if you don't have ladybird stickers to hand.

You will need (per pencil)

Pencil with rubber tip
3-D paint in yellow, red and green
Small block of modelling clay
Pencil
Scissors
Scrap of green Funky Foam
Hole punch, hammer and mat
20-cm (8-in) length of green thread
PVA glue (craft glue)
2 ladybird stickers

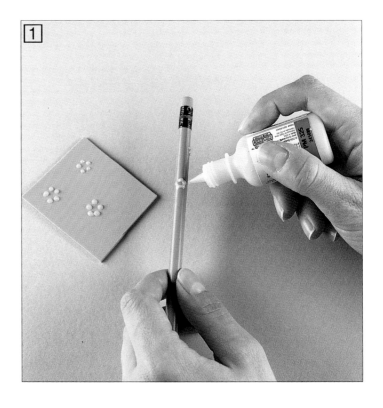

1. These pencils are decorated with 3-D paint flowers. It's a good idea to practise painting the flowers on a scrap piece of paper first. When you are happy with the result, use the yellow 3-D paint to paint five dots in a flower shape in a scattered pattern all over the pencil. The paint will take a while to dry, so press the pencil tip into a small block of play clay and leave it to dry for about one hour.

2. When the yellow flower petals are dry, add a single dot of red 3-D paint to the centre of each flower and three little leaf dots around each flower in green 3-D paint. Carefully return the pencil to the modelling clay block to dry.

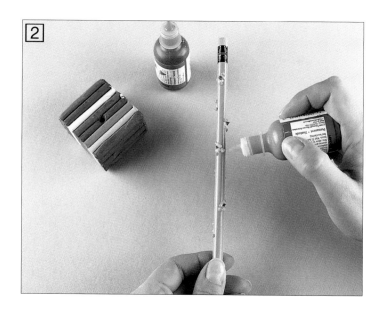

3. While the paint is drying, you can make the foam leaves. Trace the leaf template on page 90 and cut it out. Place the pattern on the piece of green Funky Foam and draw around it with a pencil. Repeat, as you will need two leaves. Carefully cut out the leaves with scissors, then ask an adult to punch a hole at one end of each leaf. To do this, place the leaves on the mat, position the hole punch near the tip of the leaf and use the hammer to make the hole.

4. Thread the length of green thread through the hole in the leaf and wind the thread around the top end of the decorated pencil. Use a little PVA glue to hold the thread in place. Finish by sticking a ladybird sticker on each leaf. If you don't have ladybird stickers, you can draw your own with red and black 3-D paints. Make sure you let the paint dry thoroughly before attaching the leaves.

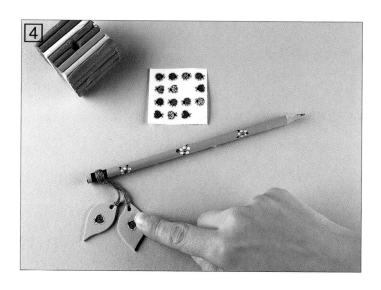

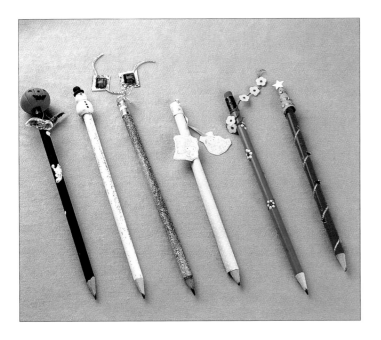

PENCIL GALLERY

★ **Halloween pencil:** I painted the pencil black and made a tiny pumpkin from orange eraser clay before gluing it onto the top end of the pencil. The ghost shapes are painted on with white 3-D paint and the bats are stickers attached to each end of a short length of thread.

★ **Snowman pencil:** this pencil has been painted white and decorated with a little silver glitter glue. The snowman is made from oven-bake clay.

★ **Wizard's pencil:** This pencil is decorated with glitter glue. Two gems are stuck onto squares of gold card then attached to lengths of gold thread which are tied onto the pencil.

★ **Flower pencil:** I decorated this pencil with bright flowers and used punched-out paper flowers glued onto a green thread to feature at the end of the pencil.

★ **Pretty in pink pencil:** I used a glue stick to attach this pretty pink gift wrap to the pencil. The stickers are attached to a short length of ribbon.

★ **Christmas pencil:** A gold string is wound round this pencil dotted with tiny gold stars. The tree is a green paper cone decorated with glitter glue, stick-on gems and sequins.

Mini project: Paper-wrapped pencils

Another way to decorate pencils is to cover them with gift wrap or coloured paper. This is quick and easy to do and you could use the same paper to cover a book or pencil box. Choose paper decorated with a small design like flowers, dots or stars. I decorated this little set of pencil crayons with star-spangled paper and I used a glue stick to attach the paper to the pencil. Be sure to apply plenty of glue to the edge of the paper so that it does not curl up when it is dry. To give a really professional finish, squeeze a little red 3-D paint on the top end of each pencil. This set of pencil crayons would make a lovely little gift for someone special.

Pencil-top snake eraser

This clever little eraser snake will slot onto the top of a pencil. Eraser clay is fun and easy to use – try making a selection of eraser snakes in different colours and styles. You will need to bake finished items in the oven to harden.

You will need

Eraser clay in pink, purple, orange, blue and green
Pencil
Permanent black marker pen

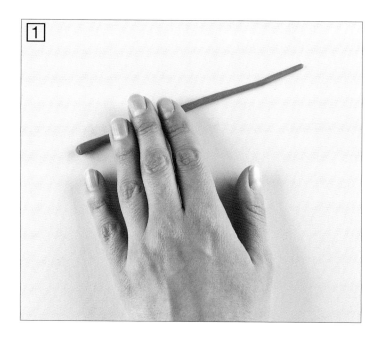

1. Take a piece of pink eraser clay the size of a medium marble and, using your fingertips, roll it into a thin sausage shape about 18 cm (7 in) long.

ADULTS: Eraser clay is a clever product that can be moulded into useful gifts. It must be baked by an adult, according to the manufacturer's instructions.

2. Now carefully wind the sausage shape around the top end of the pencil, leaving a long tail and forming a head at the top, as shown in the picture. You should be able to wind the sausage around the pencil about four times.

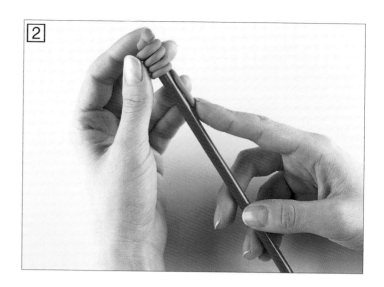

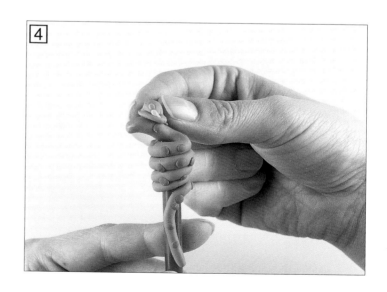

3. Decorate the snake with tiny purple dots made from little balls of eraser clay. Flatten them between your fingers and then press them gently onto the snake.

4. Make a little hat by rolling two pea-size pieces of orange eraser clay into balls and then flattening one to make the brim. Attach the other ball to the surface of the brim and gently press the hat onto the snake's head. You could decorate the hat with tiny blue, green and pink eraser clay flowers or you could even make a hat band. An adult should carefully remove the snake from the pencil and bake it according to the manufacturer's instructions. When the snake is baked and cooled, draw in eyes with the black marker pen.

Mini project: Caterpillar erasers

Meet Sim and Sue, the caterpillar erasers! These cute little caterpillars are made from eraser clay. Have fun making them then keep them on your work area ready to use. You could make a little caterpillar eraser for a friend, too. Once you have mastered working with eraser clay, try your hand at a few more designs. You could make a Christmas tree eraser or use a small shape cutter to create flower erasers, like the ones in this picture which are decorated with coloured eraser clay.

You will need
Eraser clay in green, pink, purple and yellow
Baking tray lined with aluminium foil
2 tiny wobble eyes per caterpillar
PVA glue (craft glue)

1. Knead a walnut-size piece of green eraser clay. Divide it into eight balls, each slightly larger than the other. As a guide, the head should be the size of a large pea and the smallest ball, which is the tip of the tail, should be the size of a small pea.

2. Join up the balls by pressing them lightly together to make the caterpillar. If your first caterpillar doesn't turn out so well, mash it up and start again.

3. Roll two pea-size pieces of pink clay into balls to make the hat. Flatten one to make the brim and press it gently onto the caterpillar's head. Now attach the other ball to the surface of the brim.

4. Decorate the hats with flowers made from tiny pieces of eraser clay, or a strip of clay if you are making a band, in your chosen colours.

5. Place the caterpillar on the aluminium-lined baking tray and ask an adult to bake the clay in the oven, following the manufacturer's instructions. When the clay is baked and cooled, stick on the wobble eyes with PVA glue.

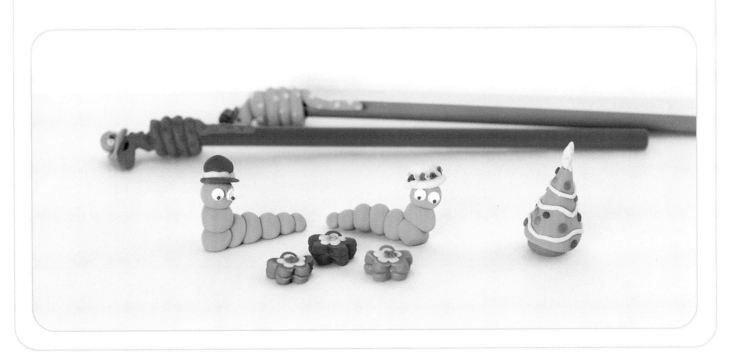

Gift box and tissue paper

Have a go at making and decorating these pretty gift boxes. If you are making a gift box for a particular present, you could decorate the box in a way that complements it. For example, if the gift were a selection of sweets, you could decorate the box with a sweet stamp. If you don't have a suitable box, see Step 1 to make your box own from card.

You will need

Little box or make your own (see Step 1):
  A4 or 8½ x 11 in piece of white cardboard
  Pencil
  Scissors
  Masking tape

Red acrylic paint
Paintbrush
Small daisy stamp
White ink pad
Yellow 3-D paint
A5 or 5½ x 8½ in sheet of red tissue paper

1. If you are making your own gift box, copy and cut out the box and lid templates on pages 90–91. Trace the outline onto the piece of cardboard, pencilling in the fold lines, too. Ask an adult to cut around the outline as cardboard can be very difficult to cut. Now score along the fold lines using the tip of the scissors to make the folding easier. Fold the sides up, then stick masking tape around the sides of the box and lid to hold them together.

2. Paint both the inside and the outside of the box and lid with red acrylic paint. You will need to paint half the box first. When the painted area is dry, hold the box on the dry painted area and paint the remaining area. While the box and lid are drying, rinse the paintbrush thoroughly under cold running water. You are now ready to decorate the box. Gently press the daisy stamp onto the white ink pad and randomly stamp the daisies onto the sides of the box and lid, re-inking the stamp as necessary.

3. When the daisies have dried, squeeze a dot of yellow 3-D paint onto the centre of the daisies. Set aside until dry.

4. While the box is drying, decorate your lining paper. Do this by stamping white daisies onto the sheet of red tissue paper, as with the box and lid, and finish with yellow 3-D paint dots in the centre of the daisies. Set aside to dry before lining your gift box with it.

Mini project: Home-made stamps

Make your own stamps from scrap pieces of Funky Foam. Here, I pressed a small star-shaped cookie cutter onto the Funky Foam to score a pattern, which I then cut out with scissors. To make the base of the stamp, cut out three squares of foam slightly larger than the star shape and stick them together with double-sided tape. Stick the star onto the base of the square. Make a small handle to stick onto the top of the squares with double-sided tape. Use the home-made stamp as you would a commercial one.

These boxes have been painted and decorated with home-made stamps. Follow the quick and easy method above to make your own stamps in whatever size and shape you want!

Friendly flowerpot and plant tag

Decorate a flowerpot and fill it with a leafy plant. These cheerful little indoor flowerpots have been painted with acrylic paint and decorated with Funky Foam faces. There are templates for the faces and hat plant tags on page 93, but you might want to try designing your own.

You will need

Small terracotta flowerpot and saucer
Red acrylic paint
Paintbrush
Pencil
Scissors
Scraps of Funky Foam in red, yellow, green and purple
PVA glue (craft glue)
2 wobble eyes

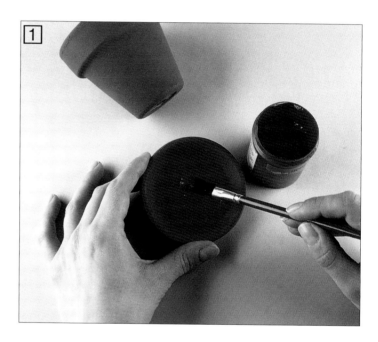

1. Paint the flowerpot and saucer with the red acrylic paint. Set the pot and saucer aside to dry and rinse the paintbrush thoroughly under cold running water.

> **TIP**
> When using paint, you may want to lay down a sheet of newspaper on your work surface before you start, just in case you make a mess!

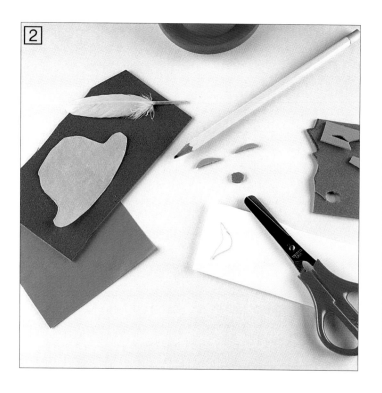

2. Copy the eyebrows, nose and mouth templates on page 93 and cut them out or draw your own. Trace around the outlines of the shapes on scraps of Funky Foam and cut them out.

3. When the painted pots are dry, use PVA glue to attach the eyes, eyebrows, nose and mouth to the flowerpots. If you don't have wobble eyes, make eyes from black and white Funky Foam or paper.

Mini project: Hat plant tag

To make a plant tag for your pot, copy the hat template on page 93, cut it out and trace the outline onto a scrap of Funky Foam and cut it out. Lay the shape flat on your work surface and use as much imagination as you can to decorate it. A brightly-coloured strip of paper makes a great hat band. I stuck on a feather, too, for a really special touch. If you do not have a feather, you could cut one from a piece of paper, or use an artificial flower instead. Use double-sided tape to attach the hat to a drinking straw and then poke the straw into the soil in the pots.

Mini project: Dotty flowerpots

These flowerpots have a stylish but simple dotty pattern. Give flowerpots and saucers an all-over coat of acrylic paint in your choice of colour and leave to dry. When the base coat is completely dry, use a small paintbrush to paint spots in a random pattern all over the pot. Practise painting spots on a scrap of paper before decorating your flowerpot.

WHAT TO GROW IN YOUR POTS

A teaspoon of grass seed sprinkled onto damp compost and watered regularly should quickly grow into a spiky hairdo, perfect to stand a hat in! You could also sow mustard or cress seeds, and even salad leaves.

Place mats

These lovely place mats are made by decorating an enlarged photograph and laminating it. Choose your favourite photograph and enlarge it on a colour photocopier. If you don't have one, you could draw a picture instead. Your local photocopy store should have a laminator if you don't have one.

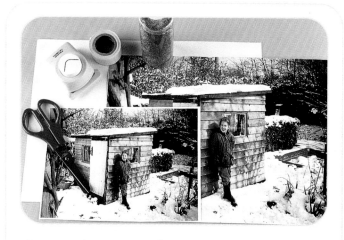

You will need

Photograph enlarged to A4 or 8½ x 11 in
Scissors
Corner cutter punch
A4 or 8½ x 11 in sheet of white paper
Double-sided tape
Silver glitter glue
Laminator

1. Trim the four edges of the A4 photograph so that it is ½ cm (¼ in) smaller all round. Use the corner cutter punch to cut round edges on the corners of the A4 sheet of white paper and the photograph. If you do not have a corner cutter punch, then round off the corners with a pair of scissors.

2. Use double-sided tape to attach the photograph centrally on the sheet of white paper. Here, the snow has been highlighted with silver glitter glue. When decorating your picture, select areas you like in particular and highlight them with glitter glue. When dry, the place mat is ready to laminate.

Snowmen place mat

A set of place mats make a great present for a grandparent. This themed place mat makes an ideal Christmas present!

You will need

A4 or 8½ x 11 in sheet of white paper
Scissors
Scrap of black paper
Double-sided tape
A4 or 8½ x 11 in sheet of red paper
A4 or 8½ x 11 in sheet of silver paper
A4 or 8½ x 11 in sheet of blue card
Photograph at A5 or 5½ x 8½ in size
Orange colouring pencil
Black felt-tip pen
Silver glitter glue
Laminator

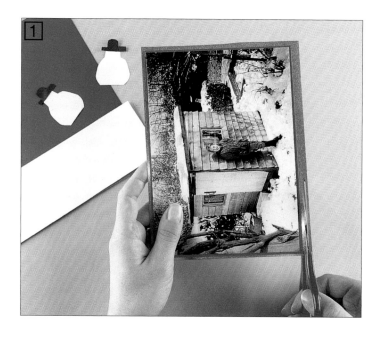

1. Cut a length of paper 5 cm (2 in) wide from the A4 white paper. This will be the snow at the bottom of the place mat. Copy the template on page 90 and cut out two snowmen from the remaining white paper and two hats from the black paper. Use double-sided tape to attach the photograph centrally on the sheet of red paper. Using scissors, cut away all but a narrow border around the photograph. Now use double-sided tape to attach the red framed picture to the silver paper and cut away all but a narrow border of silver. Set aside.

2. Use double-sided tape to attach the strip of white paper from Step 1 at the bottom of the blue card. Use double-sided tape to attach the framed photograph centrally on the place mat's base. Use double-sided tape again to attach the snowmen and their black hats and draw on orange noses and black coal eyes and mouths. Decorate the place mat with silver glitter glue to highlight areas of particular interest, such as snow, clouds or flowers. Laminate when the glue is dry.

Mini project: Greetings card

Use double-sided tape to attach your chosen photograph to a sheet of silver paper. Carefully cut around the photograph, leaving a narrow silver border. Use double-sided tape to attach the framed picture to red paper and cut around the frame leaving a narrow red border. Stick this to a third layer of blue paper, once again leaving a narrow border of blue as you cut around the frame. Stick the framed photograph onto a thin, folded card base.

Wizard's stuff

This magical wand sits in its own little frame and can be hung up on a bedroom wall. I used a length of dowel painted blue and glittered it to make this wand. You might have different ideas about how a wand should look so use the basic instructions and make a wand in your own design.

You will need

Picture frame approximately 30 x 12 cm (12 x 5 in), glass removed

A4 or 8½ x 11 in sheet of red Funky Foam
Pencil
Scissors
Double-sided tape
2 plastic stick-on hooks
A5 or 5½ x 8½ in sheet of yellow Funky Foam
25-cm (10-in) length of narrow dowel
Blue acrylic paint
Paintbrush
PVA glue (craft glue)
Gold glitter stars
Red shiny tape
Gold glitter glue

1. Start by making the frame. To do this, place the picture frame backing on the red Funky Foam and draw around it with the pencil. Cut out the shape with scissors and stick the foam to the backing with double-sided tape.

2. To assemble the picture frame, attach the stick-on hooks half way down the backing and about 5 cm (2 in) in from either side. Use your ruler and pencil to measure where they should be before you stick them on. Place the frame over the backing and secure in place.

3. You can now make the wand. Paint the dowel with blue acrylic paint. When dry, spread PVA glue on the end of the wand and sprinkle gold glitter stars over the glue. Press them down gently to make sure they stick to the wand.

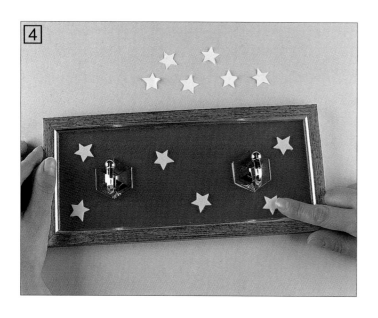

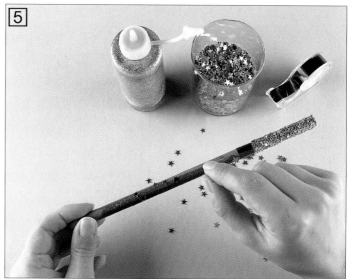

4. Copy the star template on page 93 and cut it out. Place the star shape on the yellow Funky Foam, trace around the outline with a pencil and cut it out. You will need six stars in total. Stick these onto the red backing with double-sided tape.

5. Wind a piece of red shiny tape immediately beneath the glittered section. Spread a thin layer of gold glitter glue over the rest of the wand. Finish by placing a few gold glitter stars randomly on the pencil. The glitter glue should hold these in place.

The wizard's cloak

This dashing cloak will give a budding wizard a professional air. The cloak is made from satin fabric and, when worn, it will fall from a young wizard's shoulders and swish when he twirls. The cloak could also be cut from sateen lining or any fabric that drapes well.

You will need

150 cm (59 in) of 150-cm (59-in) wide blue satin or sateen lining

150 cm (59 in) of 150-cm (59-in) wide purple satin or sateen lining

2 metres (79 in) of string

Pencil

Scissors

Thread

Sewing machine

5 cm (2 in) strip of stick-on Velcro

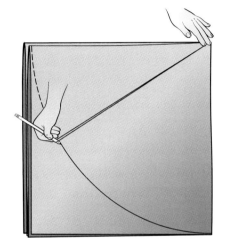

1. Fold the blue piece of fabric in half and then in half again to make a square. Fold the string in half and hold the pencil at the end of the loop. Hold the other end at the corner of the folded fabric and run the pencil around in a quarter circle along the open edges of the folded fabric. Carefully cut along the drawn line, making sure the layers of fabric remain in place. Repeat with the purple fabric.

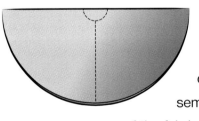

2. Open out the blue fabric so that it is folded over only once and mark a semi-circle at the centre of the fabric for the neckline (use a saucer or plate to mark the shape). Cut out the circle. Unfold the fabric. Repeat with the purple fabric.

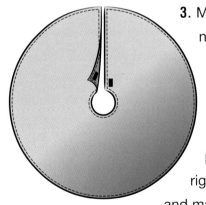

3. Make a cut from the neckline all the way down to the edge of the circle to make the opening. Repeat with the purple fabric. Lay right sides together and machine sew all around, leaving a small gap to turn the cloak through. Sew up the gap and stick on the Velcro fastener at the neck.

> **TIP**
> This dashing cloak can be decorated with cut-out stars or other magical shapes sewn onto the cloak.

Butterfly picture frame

A prettily decorated picture frame makes a great gift, and if you place a special photograph in the frame it will be well received by friends and relatives alike. You might want to decorate frames in a similar style but using your favourite colours or bedroom colour scheme.

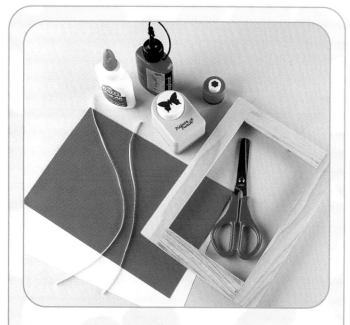

You will need

Small wooden picture frame
Red acrylic paint
Paintbrush
A4 or 8½ x 11 in sheet of white paper
Scissors
PVA glue (craft glue)
Small butterfly punch
Small flower punch
Scrap of red paper
Red 3-D paint

ADULTS: Remove the glass from the frame before giving the frame to a child. Insert the glass once the decorated frame is dry and ready for use. Younger children may need help with 3-D paint.

1. Start by painting the picture frame with red acrylic paint and set aside to dry. Cut out four 0.5-cm (¼-in) wide white paper strips slightly longer than the longest side of the frame. Stick each one down in turn with PVA glue, about 0.5 cm (¼ in) in from the outer edges of the frame. Trim off the excess with scissors.

2. Using the left-over white paper, punch out four butterflies and 20 flowers with the butterfly and flower punches. Also punch out four red butterflies. Very lightly fold the red butterflies along the body and apply a tiny dot of PVA glue on the fold line. Attach a red butterfly on each corner of the frame. It will look like the butterflies are about to fly off! Now, fold the white butterflies in the same way, apply a tiny dot of glue to the fold line and place each butterfly over the red one, making sure that some of the red butterfly underneath is still visible.

3. Stick down five white flowers around each butterfly with PVA glue. Finally, squeeze a dot of red 3-D paint in the centre of each flower and your picture frame is complete!

TIP
A decorated picture frame filled with a special photograph of you or you family would make a great gift for your grandparents or special family friends. You could get the family together for a special photo session or get a friend to take a few photos and once they are developed, choose the best one to put in the frame.

TIP
If you don't have a picture frame to hand, you can make one yourself using a piece of card for the base and the frame and a sheet of acetate instead of glass. Use double-sided tape to fix everything in place.

Above: Punched coloured paper shapes and a little humour decorate these simple picture frames. I painted the baby photo frame with bright yellow acrylic paint and decorated the edges with punched-out butterflies and flowers in pretty rainbow colours. The froggy frame is also made using a paper punch. I painted the frame blue and used strips of coloured paper to make a simple but stylish edge. The frogs are punched from thin shiny green card and attached using 3-D foam glue pads. You will recognise that the red and white frame is a mirror image of the main project.

Door name-plate

Make a smart door name-plate for your bedroom. This one is decorated with yellow and red stars. You could make a name-plate in your own style: instead of stars, cut out Funky Foam daisies or dinosaurs. If you don't have Funky Foam, use a sheet of card for the background and cut decorative shapes from coloured paper. Check with an adult before sticking it to your bedroom door!

You will need

Ruler
Pencil
Scissors
2 A4 or 8½ x 11 in sheets of yellow Funky Foam
A4 or 8½ x 11 in sheet of blue Funky Foam
Double-sided tape

1. Start by making the base. Using the ruler and pencil, measure then cut out a piece of yellow Funky Foam 20 x 15 cm (8 x 6 in) and a piece of blue Funky Foam 18.5 x 12.5 cm (7½ x 5½ in).

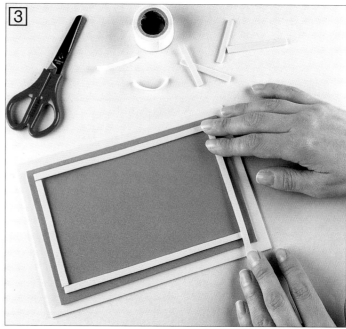

2. Lay the yellow sheet on your work surface. Use double-sided tape to attach the blue sheet centrally onto the yellow sheet. Don't stick it down firmly until you are sure it is in the centre of the yellow sheet!

3. Now you are ready to make the border. Cut two 0.5 x 17-cm (¼ x 7-in) strips of yellow foam sheet. Then cut two others 0.5 x 10.5 cm (¼ x 4 in) long. Use double-sided tape to stick them 0.5 cm (¼ in) in from the edges of the blue base.

4. Copy the star template on page 93 and cut it out. Place the shape on a left-over piece of yellow foam sheet, trace around the outline and cut out the shape. You will need 12 stars in total, three for each corner.

5. Each star has a red background so use double-sided tape to stick the yellow stars on the red foam sheet then carefully cut around each star, making sure there is a thin red border around it.

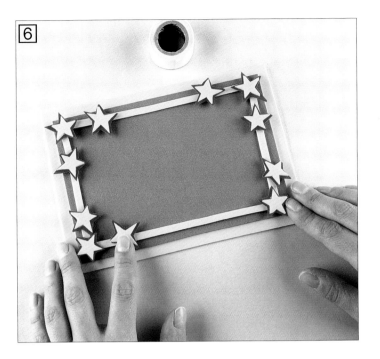

6. Use double-sided tape to attach the stars around the frame. Make sure you stick a star down over each corner to hide the unsightly join.

7. Using a pencil, draw the name for the name-plate on some red Funky Foam. Cut the letters out and use double-sided tape to stick them in place. Make sure the letters are not too big to fit on the frame! You may want to experiment with paper letters first.

Mini project: Floral name-plate

This pretty floral name plate is made using wavy-edged scissors and flower and leaf punches. Not all punches can cut through Funky Foam; you will need the scissor variety but if you don't have suitable punches, use shop-bought cut-outs or cut out the shapes with scissors. Again, use your imagination to create a design and a colour scheme that work well with your bedroom.

Sparkly bracelet

This bead encrusted bracelet is fairly easy to make. Spend a little time and design yourself a masterpiece or use stickers, glitter and sequins to produce a fun piece in just a few minutes.

You will need

Ruler

Terrifically Tacky Tape

Scissors

Embroidery thread in pink, blue and lemon braided together to form a 25-cm (10-in) length

Pink ribbon of the same width as the Terrifically Tacky Tape

Pink rosebud ribbon

Small mixed beads

Pink micro beads

2 heart-shaped beads

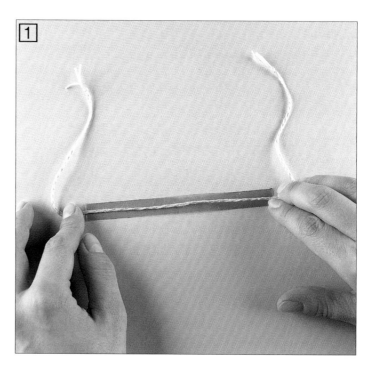

1. Measure your wrist and add 1 cm (½ in) to the measurement. For example, if your wrist measures 9 cm (3½ in), add 1 cm (½ in) to make a total of 10 cm (4 in), which will be the length of your bracelet. Measure and cut a piece of Tacky Tape to fit this measurement. Peel the backing from the tape and lay the tape down, sticky side up. Carefully place the braided thread along the centre of the tape with the tails hanging equally over the ends of the tape.

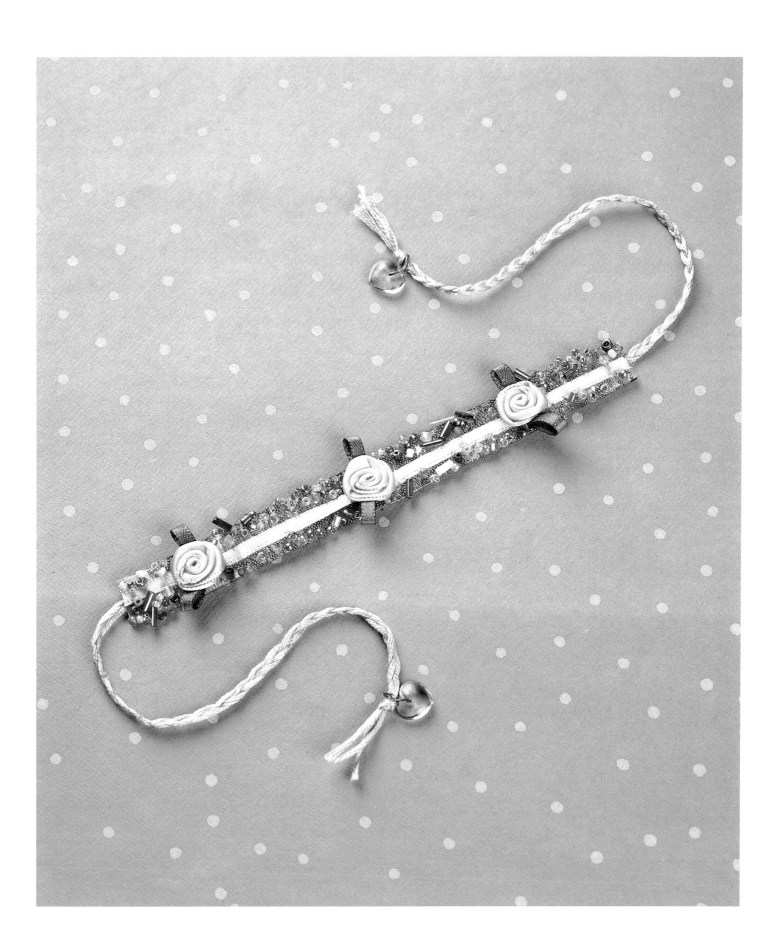

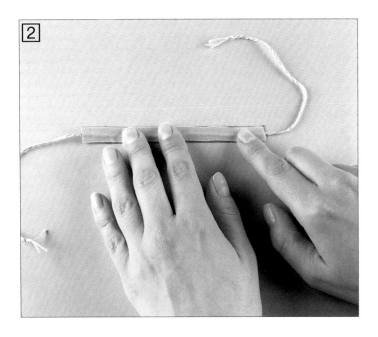

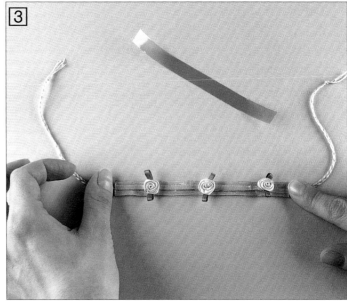

2. Measure and cut a length of pink ribbon exactly the length of the tape and lay it over the braid-covered tape. Press the ribbon down firmly in place.

3. Turn the covered tape over and peel off the backing tape from the second side. Lay a 10-cm (4-in) length of rosebud ribbon along the centre of the sticky tape.

4. Now you can decorate the bracelet with beads. Place a mixed selection of beads in a flat container and pour the beads over the tape, pressing them down with your fingers to ensure good adhesion. Sprinkle micro beads to fill any tiny gaps.

ADULTS: Encourage children to draw out their own designs before starting the project. They can begin by laying out the beads and sequins on a piece of paper before sticking down the pieces.

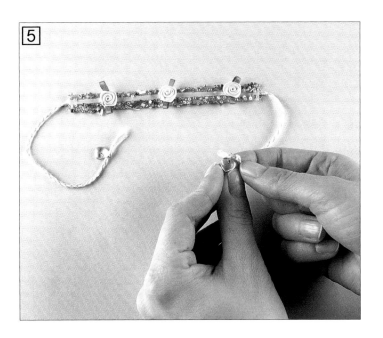

5. Finally, thread a pretty heart-shaped bead onto the end of each braid, and tie a knot in the braid to hold it fast. Your bracelet is ready to wear.

> *ADULTS: If you are unable to obtain Terrifically Tacky Tape, use quality double-sided tape instead. The finished product will not be as long lasting but the project will still make a great party activity. Double-sided tape may not be able to hold the mixed beads in place as securely, but children will be able to make a bracelet using ribbon, glitter, sequins and thread.*

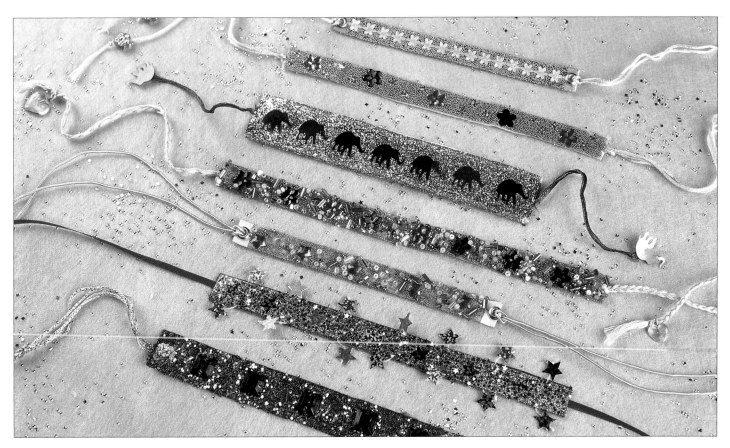

Above: Try your hand at making your own designs. You may want to sketch them on paper first. The above bracelets have all been made in the same way as the main project using a selection of beads, glitters, stick-on gems, ribbon and embroidery threads.

Secret diary

A bunch of colourful balloons decorates this beautiful book. As you turn the pages, the balloons will seem to float up. The book is made from handmade paper that has been cut, folded, bound and decorated with balloons punched from coloured sugar paper. If you don't have a balloon punch you could decorate the cover with coloured stars, flowers or maybe teddy bear shapes.

You will need

Pencil

Ruler

A3 or 11 x 17 in sheet of blue hand made paper

Paintbrush

Pot of water

8 sheets of white handmade paper cut to 15 x 28 cm (6 x 11 in)

Coloured pencil

Craft punch

15-cm (6-in) piece of string

A5 or 5½ x 8½ in sheet of white paper

Scissors

Double-sided tape

A5 or 5½ x 8½ in sheet of sugar paper in blue and yellow

A5 or 5½ x 8½ in sheet silver paper

Scraps of coloured sugar paper

Balloon punch

PVA glue (craft glue)

Blue gel pen

1. Begin by making the book cover. Use the pencil and ruler to lightly mark an area 16 x 30 cm (6½ x 12 in) on the sheet of blue handmade paper. Next, dip the paintbrush in water and generously brush a line of water along the pencil line. Make sure the water soaks through the paper to the back, then carefully tear the paper along the water line. An adult should iron the paper dry. Fold the sheet in half widthways and set aside.

2. Now make the inside pages. To do this, fold each sheet of white handmade paper in half widthways. Use a coloured pencil to mark two holes 5 cm (2 in) in from the top and bottom on the fold. Look through the base of the craft punch to ensure the hole is punched on the coloured pencil marks, as shown in the picture.

3. Mark up the next page by laying the punched page on top of it and drawing a coloured dot through the punched holes. Do this with all the pages and the cover. When marking up the cover be sure to place the inside page centrally over the cover spine. Punch out the holes.

TIP
Take a little time when making the label for your book. The method I have used here gives the label a frame for a truly professional finish. When making framed labels, choose colours that co-ordinate with the book cover and decoration. For example, a label decorated with punched-out flowers would look good on a green cover; then you could stick lines of flowers on the outer edge of each page in the book!

4. Place all the punched pages over the cover spine and thread the string through the holes, starting from the inside of the book. Tie a strong knot, followed by a bow, to hold the pages and cover in place.

ADULTS: Supervision may be required to ensure the cover and inside pages' binding holes are correctly measured and punched. It is a good idea to align the folded pages when you have cut them out, and trim the edges with scissors to ensure they are even.

5. You are now ready to make the cover label. Cut a 8 x 6-cm (3¼ x 2½-in) rectangle from the A5 sheet of white paper. Use double-sided tape to stick it onto the sheet of blue sugar paper. Using scissors, cut the blue paper, leaving a thin blue frame around the white label. Repeat with the silver and then the yellow papers. When complete, attach the label in an upper central position on the cover. Punch out six balloons from different coloured sugar papers and use PVA glue to stick them in place on the label. To complete the cover, use the blue gel pen and ruler to draw strings hanging down from the balloons.

6. Open out the book and on the first page stick a punched-out balloon at the bottom of the outer edge and, using a gel pen, draw a string from the bottom of the balloon to the edge of the page. Continue this through the book, sticking the balloon slightly higher on each page until it flies off the page, and your book is finished.

Mini project: Baby album

This pretty little baby album is made in the same way as the blue book. Use a sheet of white handmade paper as a cover and attach stickers, punched-out flowers and hearts, or sequins and glitter stars to decorate the cover. Apply a layer of aerosol glue and stick down a sheet of fine, white tissue paper over the top and trim to fit. Bind the book with a length of gauzy ribbon.

Dolly bag

Every girl needs a handbag or purse! These little bags are decorated with air-drying clay, dolly faces, sequins and glitter. If you don't have any modelling clay, you could paint or draw a face on a large button instead. An adult will need to make the bag.

You will need

Needle and thread
70 cm (28 in) green ribbon

36 x 36-cm (14 x 14-in) square of
   plain white calico fabric
Small piece of air-drying clay in white
   and brown
Permanent black marker pen
Red pencil
PVA glue (craft glue)
Small scrap of patterned fabric
Pencil
Scissors
Glitter glue in green and lilac
3-D paint in pink, blue, red and yellow
Selection of colourful charms, sequins
   and gems

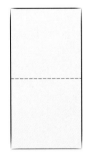

The bag is simple to make but should be made by an adult. If you have a sewing machine, use it to sew the seams, otherwise use a small running stitch. Follow the diagrams above to cut a pattern from plain white calico fabric. Fold the bag into shape and sew up either side. Fold a hem at the top and sew a length of ribbon around the edge. Finally, sew a further length of ribbon as a strap.

Dolly bag ★ 53

1. Begin by making the dolly face and hair using the air-drying clay. Roll the white clay into a ball and flatten it. Shape the brown clay into a hair do. Draw on a face using the black marker pen for the eyes and the red pencil for the cheeks and mouth. Set aside to dry: this will take a whole day.

2. Use PVA glue to stick the dolly face and hair in place on the bag. The face should be positioned about two-thirds of the way up. Copy the dress template on page 93, cut it out then place the shape on a scrap of patterned fabric. Draw around the outline with a pencil and cut out the shape with the scissors. Stick the dress down with PVA glue.

3. Squeeze a loopy pattern of green glitter glue on either side of the dolly and along the bottom edge of the bag, as shown in the picture. This will be the greenery of the bushes and grass.

4. Now squeeze on arms and legs using the pink 3-D paint and when these are dry, squeeze on some blue shoes. Be very careful not to smudge the glitter or the paints. It is best to wait until these are completely dry before moving onto the next step.

5. Squeeze a squiggly pattern of lilac glitter glue across the top half of the bag to make the sky. Add dots of red and yellow 3-D paint here and there to make flowers. Set aside to dry.

6. Randomly attach a selection of charms, sequins and gems with PVA glue to the bushes and grass areas. Leave the bag in a safe place to dry overnight before using it.

You don't have to make decorative bits and pieces for bags as there is a wide selection of ready-made braids, motifs, charms, buttons and beads available to buy.

The larger bag is decorated with frog, butterfly and dolly motifs I found in a craft store. They are attached to the bag with PVA glue and the bag is then decorated with coloured glitter glues and 3-D paints.

The smaller bag is decorated with a princess face charm I cut from a hair clip. Keep a look-out for pretty charms and motifs when out shopping.

Paper bead necklace

Paper beads are made by rolling up strips of paper around a stick or drinking straw and sticking the ends down with glue. When the glue has dried, simply remove the bead from the straw and thread it into a necklace or bracelet. You can make different shaped beads by cutting the paper strips into different shapes. Use brightly coloured sugar paper to create dazzling beads.

You will need

Ruler

Pencil

Scissors

Sheets of A3 or 11 x 17 in coloured sugar paper and gold paper

Drinking straw

Glue stick

A4 or 8½ x 11 in sheet of card

Elastic thread

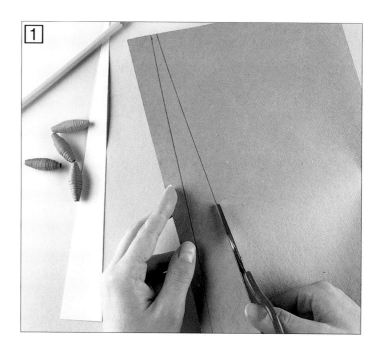

1. To make the oval beads, trace a pattern from the oval bead template on pages 92–93. Cut out the template and use it to outline some oval bead shapes on coloured sugar paper. Cut out the shapes with scissors.

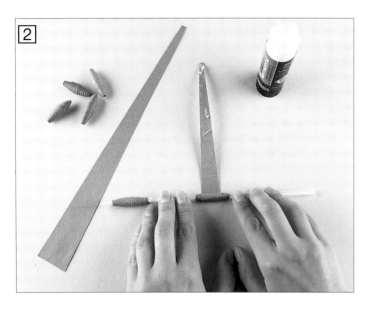

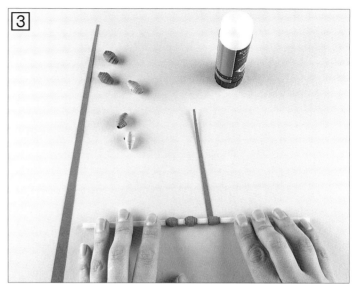

2. To make the bead, start by rolling the wider end of the paper around a drinking straw. When the paper has been completely rolled up,use glue to stick down the thinner end to hold the bead shape firmly in place. Gently slip the bead off the straw.

3. To make the round beads, use the template on pages 92–93 and make in exactly the same way as the oval beads.

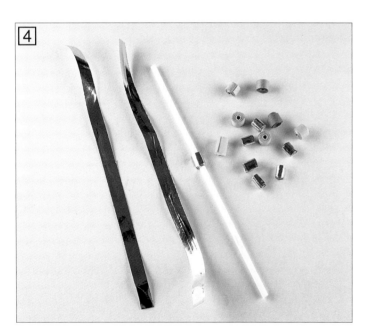

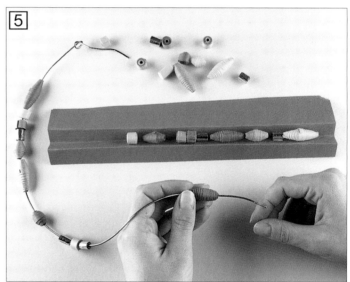

4. The gold beads are made from long strips of gold paper (about 1-cm/¼-in wide) rolled around a drinking straw and held firmly in place with glue.

5. Make a bead holder from the sheet of card. To do this, make a concertina fold (as if you were making the beginning of a folded fan). Lay your beads along the fold, arranging them until you are happy with your design, then thread the beads onto a length of elastic thread and tie a double knot to secure in place.

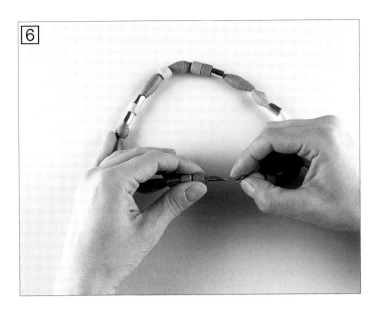

6. Thread the ends of the knot back through the beads to give a neat finish to your necklace. Your necklace is now ready to wear. You could make a pretty gift box in which to store your necklace. See pages 20–23 for inspiration.

If you don't make quite enough beads for a necklace, why not make a bracelet instead?

This little bracelet is made from rolled-up strips of coloured sugar paper and each bead is wrapped in a thin strip of gold paper for a really stylish finish. You can even paint or varnish beads or make them out of patterned gift wrap. Have fun experimenting!

Christmas decorations

Christmas decorations are great fun and easy to make. Garlands are best made from crêpe paper, which comes in lots of colours and is stocked in most craft and stationery shops. Use staples to join crêpe paper as sticky tape doesn't hold very well.

You will need

A5 or 5½ x 8½ in sheet of green paper
Pencil
Ruler
Scissors
Craft punch
Two 10-cm (4-in) lengths of gold thread
Sticky tape
Crêpe paper in green and yellow
Stapler
Double-sided tape

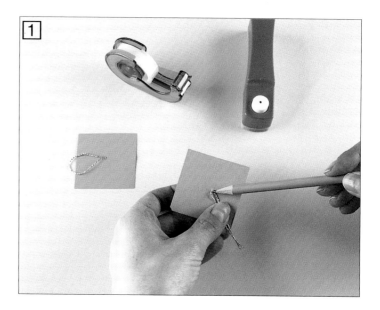

1. Start by making the paper garlands. Begin by making the paper ends. Use the pencil and ruler to measure up two 5-cm (2-in) squares of green paper and cut them out. Make a hole at the centre of each square with the craft punch and thread the looped gold thread through the hole, using the tip of a pencil to help you. Use sticky tape to hold the ends firmly in place.

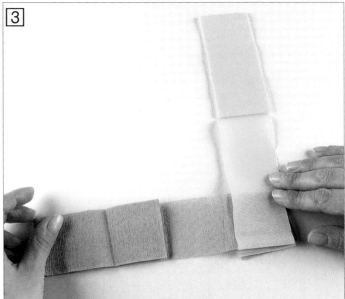

2. Use a pencil and ruler to measure 4-cm (1½-in) widths of green and yellow crêpe paper (the length of these will depend on how much crêpe paper you have). Cut along the pencil lines with scissors. Lay the green crêpe paper strip on your work surface, then lay the yellow strip over the green one at right angles. Hold in place with four staples.

3. Fold the green strip over the yellow strip, then fold the yellow strip over the green one. Repeat until all the paper is used up.

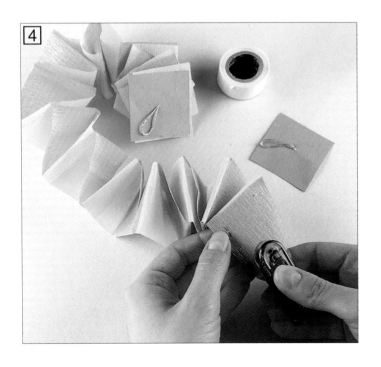

> **TIP**
> Follow the above instructions to make a short length of garland. To make a longer garland, you will need to join the crêpe paper with staples. Sticky tape or glue may not be strong enough.

4. When you have finished the folding, hold the ends in place with four staples. Use double-sided tape to stick the square green paper ends from Step 1 neatly in place. Gently pull out your completed decoration.

Glitter baubles

Did you know you could make a ball from a sheet of paper? These Christmas tree baubles are made from paper and a couple of paper fasteners! Decorate the paper with glitter glue, and when it is dry, follow the instructions to make a set of beautiful decorations for your Christmas tree. You might want to make a set for a special friend, too!

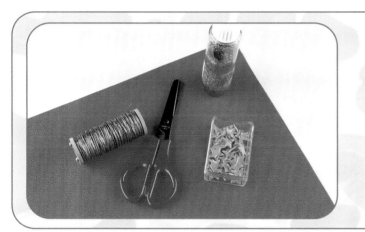

You will need

A4 or 8½ x 11 in sheet of red paper
Gold glitter glue
Scissors
Hole punch
4 star-shaped paper fasteners
Thin gold wire or thread

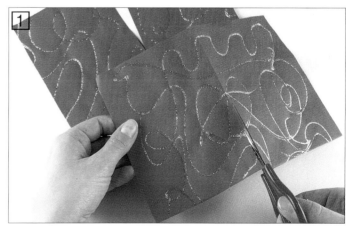

1. Squeeze a swirly pattern of gold glitter glue over the sheet of red paper and set it aside to dry overnight. When the paper is dry, fold the sheet in half lengthways, open it out and cut along the fold line to make two pieces of paper.

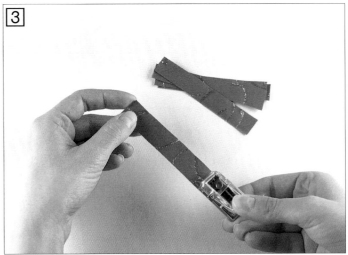

2. Take one of the pieces of paper and fold it widthways into a fan. Each fold should be about 2.5 cm (1 in) wide. Cut along each fold line. You will have eight strips of paper. Repeat with the other piece of paper.

3. Stack eight strips together and use the hole punch to make a hole about 1 cm (½ in) in from either end of the strips. You should be able to punch three or four strips at a time.

4. Push a star-shaped paper fastener through the hole at one end of the stack of strips. Make sure the fastener is inserted so that the star is on the decorated side of the paper. Turn the strips over and open out the fastener to hold the stack together. Repeat at the other end.

5. Carefully open out the fastened strips, pulling them gently round to form a ball, as shown in the photograph.

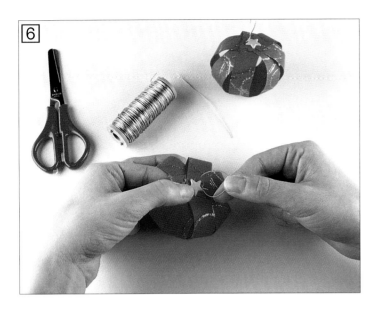

6. Attach a loop of thin wire or thread to the head of the paper fastener, winding it round neatly. You have made a sparkly Christmas tree bauble!

OTHER IDEAS
Use brightly coloured gift wrap instead of glittered paper to make festive baubles. Older children might use rivets instead of paper fasteners. Yarn or ribbon could then be threaded through the bauble.

Mini project: Sparkly bauble

You will need
2 red paper circles 7.5 cm (3 in) in diameter
Glue stick
Hole punch
Star-shaped paper fastener
A5 or 5½ x 8½ in sheet of green paper
Scissors
Coloured dot stickers
Gold thread
Gold glitter glue
Gold stars

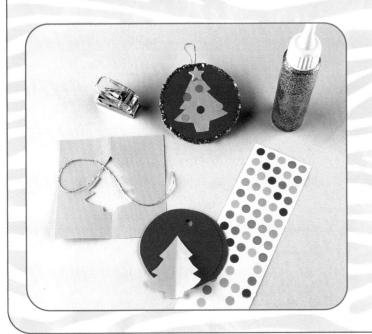

Younger children will really enjoy making this simple but effective double-sided Christmas tree bauble. Each decoration is made with two circles. Use the glue stick to stick together the red paper circles. Punch a hole with the hole punch about 1 cm (1⁄2 in) in from the edge of the circle. Insert the star-shaped paper fastener through the hole and open it out to secure it in place. Use the Christmas tree template on page 90 and cut out two Christmas tree shapes from the green paper. Stick one on either side of the circle, immediately beneath the star. Decorate the tree with dot stickers. Tie a loop of gold thread around the star fastener. Finally, apply gold glitter glue around the edge of the circle and dip it into the gold stars. Hang up to dry overnight.

Space-age mobile

Shapes cut out of Funky Foam stay fairly rigid and keep their shape well but if you don't have Funky Foam to hand, use card as thick as you can cut. You could paint the pattern directly onto the card or stick on coloured paper shapes. Mobiles look great hanging up in a window or from your bedroom ceiling. If your bedroom has a special theme, you might want to design your own mobile.

You will need

Pencil

Scissors

A5 or 5½ x 8½ in sheet of Funky Foam in purple, blue, red, green and white

PVA glue (craft glue)

Hole punch, hammer and mat

Reel of light blue cotton thread

140 cm (55 in) of thin craft wire

1. Copy the spaceship templates on page 95 and cut out the shapes. Place each template on the relevant Funky Foam sheet and trace around it with a pencil then cut out the shapes with the scissors. You will need:

1 purple spaceship	4 red wings
2 yellow bodies	2 green bases
2 blue tips	2 white clouds of smoke
4 blue windows	8 yellow stars

2. Remember that you will need to decorate both sides of the spaceship. Use PVA glue to attach the decorations on one side of the spaceship, as in the picture. Let the glue dry on one side before decorating the other side.

3. Use the hole punch, hammer and mat to make a hole in the wing of the spaceship. Also make a hole in each star. Fold a piece of 40-cm (16-in) thread in half and thread the loop through the hole of each star and make a knot to tie the ends together. Repeat for the spaceship, making sure the thread is longer than the thread hanging the stars.

TIP
Mobiles are a little fiddly to construct so take your time and be sure to make the hangers even. When you make holes in the decorative pieces, check that they are in the top centre of the piece to ensure that each piece hangs attractively.

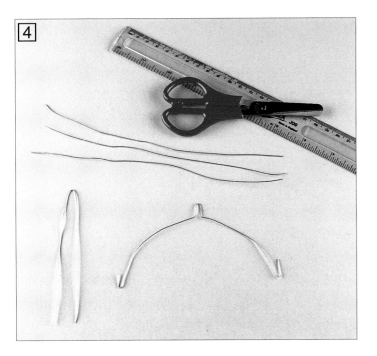

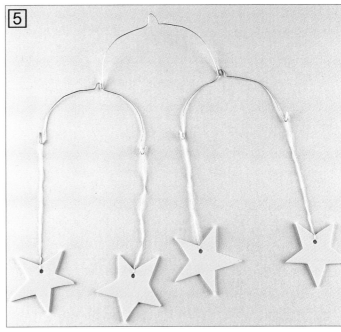

4. To make each of the mobile hangers you will need a piece of craft wire 20 cm (8 in) long. Fold the wire in half, hold the fold and gently pull each end back. Now bend each end of the wire in a curved shape and make a hook at each end. Look at the picture carefully before beginning. You will need seven hangers in total.

5. To assemble the mobile, first hang a star at either end of four hangers then lay these flat on your work surface. Hook two of these star hangers onto one of the remaining hangers and repeat with the two remaining star hangers. Finally, hook these two hangers onto the top hanger. Hang the spaceship from the top hanger.

Mini project: Flying sheep

This sheep mobile uses the same method but we made sheep instead of spaceships and stars. Draw the sheep body shapes onto white Funky Foam or thin card. Cut them out carefully and make holes to thread the string through. Cut out black legs and faces and use PVA paint to stick them to the bodies. You could make a mobile that matched your bedroom colour scheme or invent a new design for a special friend.

Space-age mobile ★ 69

Stock car

This model car will take a little time and effort to make, but painting it will be great fun. Let your imagination take over and paint or stick on wonderful flames along the sides of the car, or flying fish, birds, or whatever takes your fancy!

You will need

Pencil

A4 or 8½ x 11 in sheet of thick card

Scissors

Hole punch, hammer and mat

A4 or 8½ x 11 in sheet of thin card

Ruler

Narrow double-sided tape

2 drinking straws

Lime green acrylic paint

Paintbrush

Block of black modelling clay
  or 4 bottle lids

2 wooden skewers

A5 or 5½ x 8½ in sheet of white paper

A5 or 5½ x 8½ in sheet of black paper

A5 or 5½ x 8½ in sheet of silver paper

PVA glue (craft glue)

Tissue paper in purple
  and pink

Silver paint

Sticky tape

2 large wobble eyes

3-D paint in red and yellow

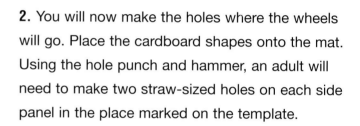

1. Copy the side panel template on page 92 and cut it out. Place the shape onto the thick card and trace around it twice to make two shapes. Make sure you also mark up the two holes where the wheels will go. Use sturdy scissors to cut out the shapes.

2. You will now make the holes where the wheels will go. Place the cardboard shapes onto the mat. Using the hole punch and hammer, an adult will need to make two straw-sized holes on each side panel in the place marked on the template.

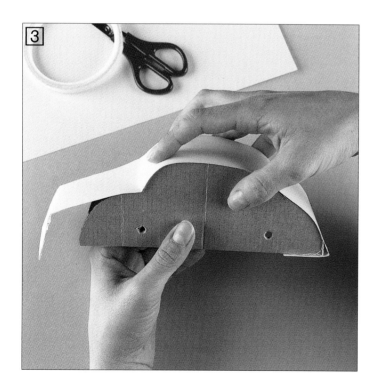

3. Measure and cut out a piece of thin card 6 x 30 cm (2½ x 12 in) for the car body. Stick a line of narrow double-sided tape along the edges of each car panel. Peel off the backing from one panel and carefully mould the cut-out thin card around the contours of the panel, starting on the underside of the car and working your way round, as shown in the picture. When this has been done, repeat with the other side panel.

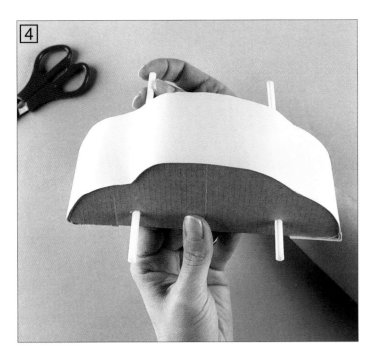

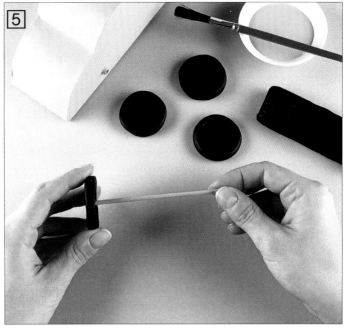

4. Push drinking straws through the holes to form the axle pipes where the wheels will go. Trim the straws with scissors so that they are flush with the sides of the car. Keep the excess pieces of straw as you will need them to make the exhaust pipes. Measure and cut out a 6 x 18 cm (2½ x 7 in) rectangle from the remaining thick card for the car base. Turn the car upside down and attach the car base using double-sided tape.

5. Paint the whole car lime green and set aside to dry. In the meantime, make the wheels. You will need four walnut-size pieces of black modelling clay. For each wheel, roll a piece into a ball and then flatten it, making sure the edges of the wheel are smooth and regular. Test each wheel out by rolling the flattened shape on its edge along your work surface to check the wheels are round and roll smoothly. Repeat for the other three wheels. Make a small indentation with a skewer in the centre of each wheel, making sure not to push the skewer all the way through. Set the wheels aside until they are hard or bake according to the manufacturer's instructions.

ADULTS: Younger children will need assistance with this project. This car can be made using grocery carton card which an older child can cut with sturdy scissors. You can also use sponge board for a neater result but an adult will need to cut out the car shapes with a craft knife. Be sure to follow recommended safety procedures and always cut against a steel ruler. **NEVER ALLOW CHILDREN TO USE A CRAFT KNIFE.**

6. Copy the window templates on page 92 and cut out the shapes. You will need one windscreen, two side windows and one back window. Place the shapes on the sheet of white paper, trace around them and cut them out. Stick the cut-out shapes on the black paper and cut around them, leaving a narrow border. Now stick the layered shapes on the silver paper and cut around them, again leaving a narrow border.

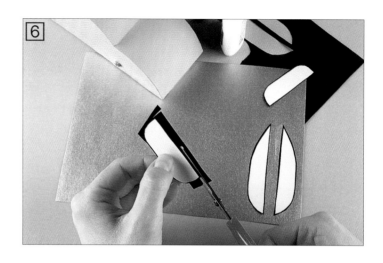

7. Stick the windows in place with PVA glue. Copy the flame templates on page 92 and cut out the shapes. Place the shapes on the purple tissue paper, trace around them and cut them out. Stick the cut-out shapes on the pink tissue paper and cut around them, leaving a narrow border. Now stick the layered shapes on the remaining white paper and cut around them, again leaving a narrow border. You will need two sets of flames, one for each side of the car. Use PVA glue to stick the flames to the sides of the car.

8. With the left-over pieces of straw from Step 4, cut and attach two pieces of drinking straw painted silver to the rear underside of the car with sticky tape. These will act as exhaust pipes. Now mark and cut two pieces of skewer so that they are 1 cm (½ in) longer than the width of the car. Apply a dot of PVA glue to the wheel indentations made in Step 5 then push the skewer in the hole and set aside so that it dries firmly in place. When dry, insert the skewer through the straw, apply a dot of glue to the other wheel and push it against the skewer and hold for a few minutes to make sure it sticks in place. Repeat for the other set of wheels.

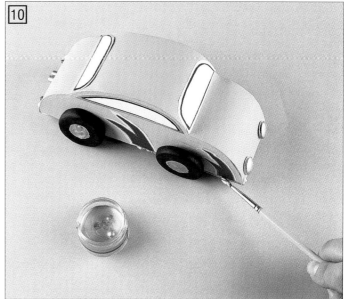

9. Stick down the two large wobble eyes in place with PVA glue to act as headlights. If you don't have wobble eyes, use small discs of card to make the lights or just paint them on.

10. Add the finishing touches by painting the headlights silver. Also paint a silver strip at the base of the car. Finally, dot on red and yellow 3-D paint at the rear of the car to act as brake and indicator lights.

Flashy 50s style

This car is made in much the same way as the stock car. Have a look around at cars when you are out. Look at their profiles. When you get home, make a pattern of a profile of a car you liked and use that to make up your own design. Once you have cut two profiles from card, follow the instructions for the main project and you should, with some practice, be able to construct a car to your own design. You could make the wheels from milk carton lids painted black.

Fairy wings, wand and crown

Every little girl needs a pair of fairy wings, a wand and a crown. Making a pair of fairy wings can sometimes be quite an involved process but I have taken a large sheet of thick, handmade watercolour paper and turned it into the prettiest set of wings and fairy crown.

You will need

A2 or 17 x 22 in sheet of 210 gsm green handmade paper
Pencil
Scissors
Paintbrush and pot of water

Heart-shaped punch
Star-shaped punch
Gold foil chocolate wrapper
Scraps of decorative paper
PVA glue (craft glue)
Stick-on gems in turquoise and green
Pink glitter and shimmer glitter
12-cm (5-in) strip of stick-on Velcro
30-cm (12-in) length of narrow dowel
White acrylic paint
Emery board
1 m (39 in) of 0.5-cm (¼-in) wide pink ribbon
2 small bells
A3 or 11 x 17 in sheet of white paper
Length of thin ribbon
Stapler

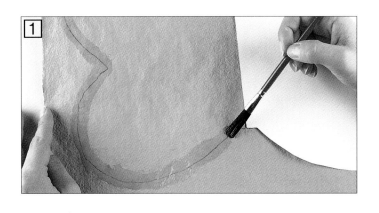

1. Start by making the wings. Copy and cut out the wing template on page 94. Lay the pattern on a sheet of green handmade paper and trace around the template in light pencil marks. Flip the template over and position it so that you get a mirror image of the wing you have just traced, trace around the template again: you now have a set of wings. Use a paintbrush and plenty of water to wet the pencil lines thoroughly.

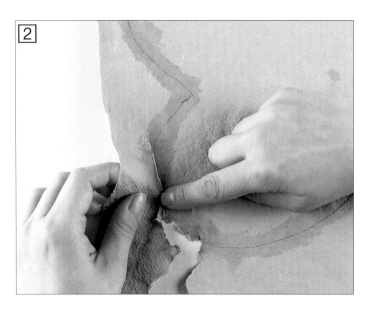

2. When the paper is thoroughly wet, carefully tear along the watermark, so cutting out the wings with a pretty, jagged edge, then set aside to dry.

3. Cut heart and star shapes from the foil and scraps of decorative paper. Use PVA glue to stick these down to decorate the wings along with some stick-on gems and glitter.

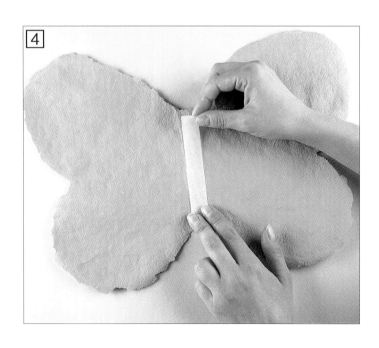

4. Attach the hook side of the stick-on Velcro to the undecorated side of the wings. Set the wings aside as you will now make the wand.

5. To make the wand, paint the length of dowel with white acrylic paint. Use an emery board to carve a 1-cm (½-in) slit across the top of one end into which the star will be wedged and glued. Copy and cut out the star template on page 93. Lay the pattern on a left-over piece of green handmade paper and cut out the shape. Run a fine line of PVA glue around the edges of the star and sprinkle with pink glitter.

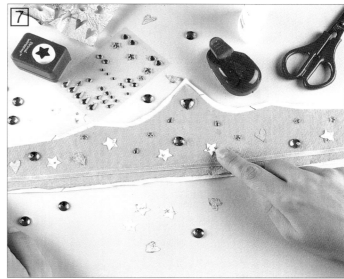

6. Glue the star firmly in place on the dowel. Wind the pink ribbon around the dowel and tie it securely in place beneath the star with a double knot. Attach a small bell to the ends of each ribbon which will tinkle when the wand is waved about.

ADULTS: As the hook side of the Velcro is attached to the wings, the loop side should be stuck on a pretty top. The wings will attach to this.

7. To make the fairy crown, copy and cut out the crown template on pages 92–93. Lay the pattern on a left-over piece of green handmade paper and trace around the template. Flip the template over and position it so that you get a mirror image of the crown you have just traced and trace around the template again: you now have a full crown. Cut out the shape and stick it onto the sheet of white paper with double-sided tape. Cut around the shape leaving a narrow white border. Decorate the crown with stars and heart shapes, gems and ribbon.

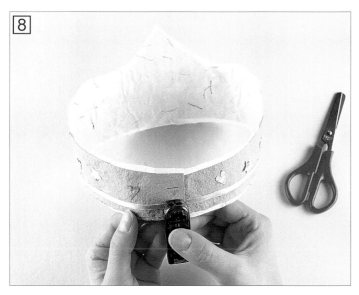

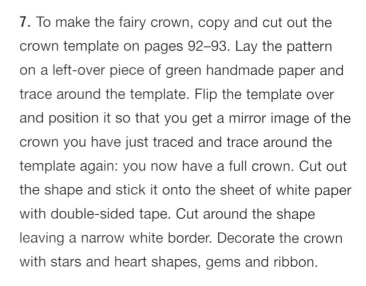

8. Measure the crown around your little girl's head. Mark the spot, remove the crown from the child's head and use staples to join the ends at the marked spot. Cut away any excess crown and put a piece of sticky tape over the staples so that the wire ends won't scratch.

Fairy wings, wand and crown ★ 79

Miniature garden and pet

Follow these simple instructions and you will be the proud owner of your own miniature garden and shaggy dog. You could make a little garden and dog house in almost any style or shape. In winter, you could make your pet a winter garden with snow. If you are not keen on dogs, you could make a little rabbit and a garden for it to live in instead.

You will need

18-cm (7-in) square of thick card
Pencil
Ruler

Scissors
Regular double-sided tape
23-cm (9-in) square of green felt
Narrow double-sided tape
2 strips of brown card 3 x 30 cm (1¼ x 12 in)
Wavy scissors
PVA glue (craft glue)
A4 or 8½ x 11 in sheet of green Funky Foam
Ripple-edge scissors
Scraps of Funky Foam in brown, red, yellow
    and orange
Daisy punch
Scraps of coloured paper
3-D paint in yellow and red
A5 or 5½ x 8½ in sheet of yellow card
A5 or 5½ x 8½ in sheet of red corrugated card
Leaf punch

1. Begin by making the base. Stick regular double-sided tape around the edges of the square of thick card. Peel off the backing from the tape and lay it sticky-side down onto the centre of the square of green felt. Use scissors to cut away the corners of the felt. Now stick double-sided tape around the edges of the card and peel away the backing, as shown in the photograph. Fold the felt edges onto the tape, making sure the felt is well stretched across the card.

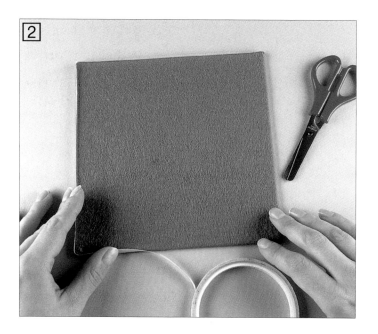

2. Turn right side up. You now have a grassy garden. Stick a line of narrow double-sided tape around three side edges of the garden and peel off the backing.

TIP
If you don,t have all the bits and pieces to construct this garden, you could recycle a shallow container by painting it and decorating it with paper or silk flowers, or flowers and bushes cut out of an old magazine.

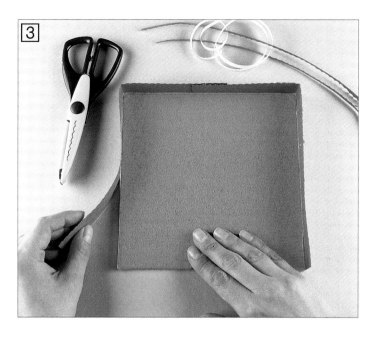

3. To make the fence, use wavy scissors to cut a pattern along the top of the two strips of brown card. Attach them to the double-sided tape, folding the strips around three sides of the garden. There will be a slight overlap at the back of the garden, so use PVA glue to stick the pieces together.

4. Now make the bushes that will decorate the hedge. Cut three 3 x 18-cm (1¼ x 7-in) strips of green Funky Foam. Use the ripple-edge scissors to cut a hedge pattern along the top edges. Stick the strips on the inside of the fence with double-sided tape.

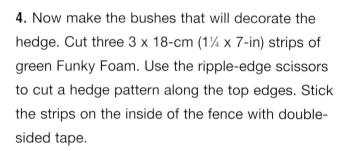

5. Cut out a tree top and three shrubs from the left-over green Funky Foam and a tree trunk from a scrap of brown Funky Foam. You might want to use the templates on page 91. Punch out flowers from red paper using the daisy punch and randomly stick them over the shrubs with dots of PVA glue. Dot a little yellow 3-D paint at the centre of the flowers. When the paint has dried, squeeze some PVA glue along the bottom edge of the tree trunk and the bottom edges of the shrubs and stick them in place, at the back corners of the garden.

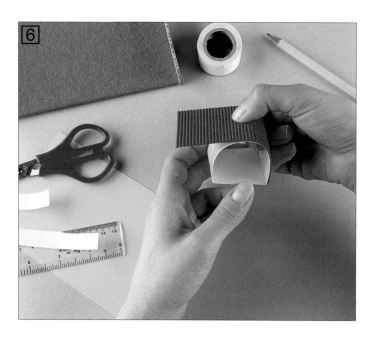

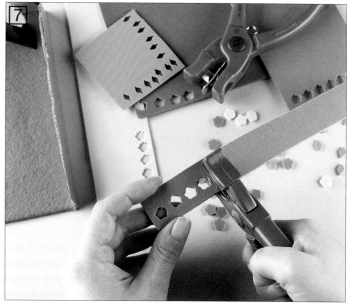

6. To make the dog house, trace the template on page 91 and cut out the shape. Place the shape on the sheet of yellow card, making sure you mark up all the fold lines. Cut out the shape and fold along the fold lines, using a strip of double-sided tape to hold it in place. Next, cut a piece of corrugated red card 11 x 6 cm (4¼ x 2½ in) and stick it on the curved part of the house with double-sided tape. Now use a strip of double-sided tape to stick the dog house firmly in place in the garden.

7. Punch out a selection of leaf and flower shapes with the leaf and flower punches from your choice of coloured Funky Foam. This is a great way of using up small scraps of Funky Foam.

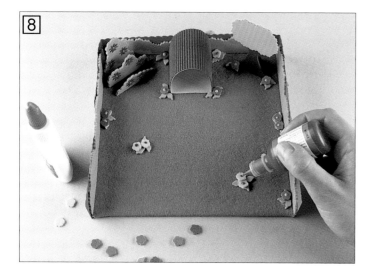

8. Decorate the garden with the leaves and flowers from Step 7. Use spots of PVA glue to hold them in place and a small dot of red or yellow 3-D paint to mark the centre of the flowers.

ADULTS: Making a pet from polymer clay can be fun but may be challenging for younger children. If this is the case, why not buy a toy model of a dog or cat and encourage your child to make a home for it. Polymer clay needs to be baked in a kitchen oven and an adult will need to do this.

Mini project: Shaggy dog

You will need

Polymer clay in grey (or black and white) and pink

Garlic press

Modelling tool

Scissors

2 small brown beads

1 black bead

1. Roll a sausage shape 2.5 cm (1 in) long and about 1 cm (½ in) in diameter from the grey polymer clay. Make the sausage slightly pointed at one end. Set aside.

2. Use the garlic press to make the dog's coat. Place a walnut-size lump of grey clay in the press and push through. Use a modelling tool to lift the clay 'threads' off the press and gently lay them onto the dog's back, pressing them down gently along the line of the back. Use a few short pieces to make a fringe.

3. Trim away any excess coat with scissors. Make four little balls for the dog's paws and press them into place. Press two brown beads into place for the eyes and a single black bead for the nose.

4. Finally, roll out a thin sausage shape about 4 cm (1½ in) long from the pink clay and make a bow. Press it onto the dog's head.

I also made my little dog a bowl and bone from air-drying clay.

Doll's house and furniture

This roomy doll's house can be made in an afternoon. Choose pretty coloured gift wrap or wallpaper ends to decorate the walls. If you can't get hold of sponge board, use a double thickness of grocery carton cardboard instead. Once your doll's house is finished, why not make some miniature furniture?

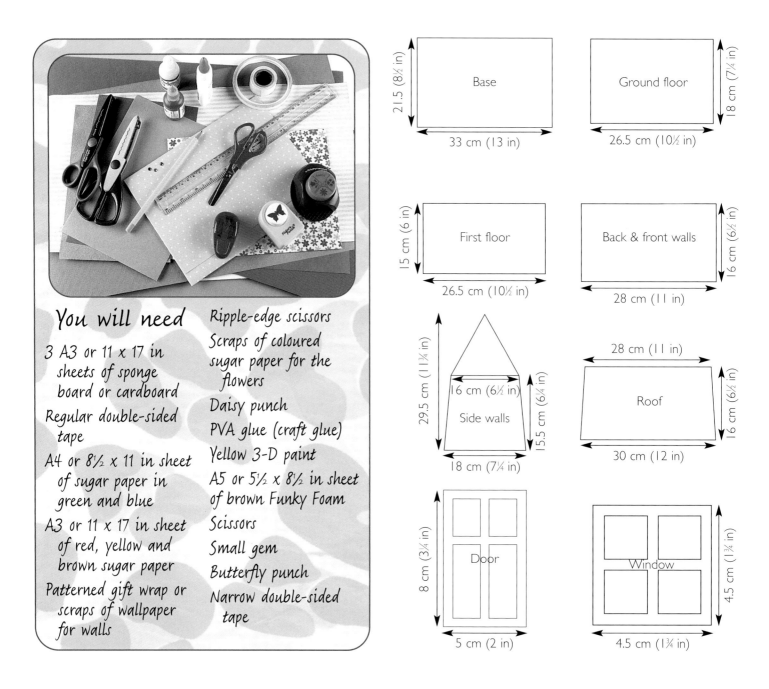

You will need

3 A3 or 11 x 17 in sheets of sponge board or cardboard

Regular double-sided tape

A4 or 8½ x 11 in sheet of sugar paper in green and blue

A3 or 11 x 17 in sheet of red, yellow and brown sugar paper

Patterned gift wrap or scraps of wallpaper for walls

Ripple-edge scissors

Scraps of coloured sugar paper for the flowers

Daisy punch

PVA glue (craft glue)

Yellow 3-D paint

A5 or 5½ x 8½ in sheet of brown Funky Foam

Scissors

Small gem

Butterfly punch

Narrow double-sided tape

Base — 21.5 (8½ in) × 33 cm (13 in)

Ground floor — 18 cm (7¼ in) × 26.5 cm (10½ in)

First floor — 15 cm (6 in) × 26.5 cm (10½ in)

Back & front walls — 16 cm (6½ in) × 28 cm (11 in)

Side walls — 29.5 cm (11¾ in) / 16 cm (6½ in) / 15.5 cm (6¼ in) / 18 cm (7¼ in)

Roof — 28 cm (11 in) / 16 cm (6½ in) / 30 cm (12 in)

Door — 8 cm (3¼ in) × 5 cm (2 in)

Window — 4.5 cm (1¾ in) × 4.5 cm (1¾ in)

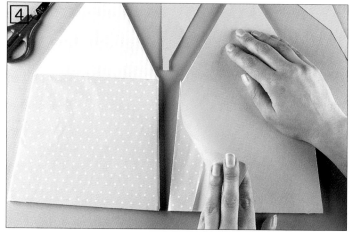

1. Measure and cut out all the pattern pieces on page 86 from sponge board or grocery carton cardboard. Begin with the base of the house. Stick regular double-sided tape around the edges of the base. Peel off the backing from the tape and lay the base, sticky-side down, on the centre of the green sugar paper. Cut away the corners of the paper and fold the edges over onto the sticky tape to hold firm.

2. Cover the ground floor piece in the same way with the brown sugar paper. Use double-sided tape to attach the floor to the base. Make sure the floor is centrally positioned along one long edge of the base.

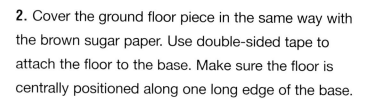

3. Cover the first-floor piece with brown sugar paper on one side and your chosen wall covering on the other, trimming away any excess paper with scissors.

4. Cover the outer back and side walls with yellow sugar paper. Turn the pieces over to decorate the inner walls. Cover the ground floor and the first floor with your chosen wall coverings. Here we have used a yellow polka dot covering for the ground floor and a blue and white stripy paper for the first floor. Cover the inner side of the roof with decorative paper and the outer side with red sugar paper.

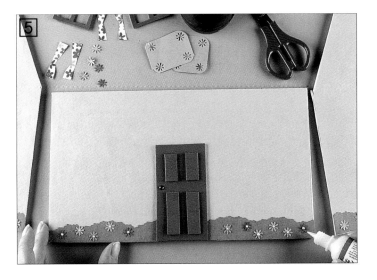

5. Decorate the bottom of the outer front and side walls of the house with strips of green sugar paper cut along the top edge with the ripple-edge scissors to give an impression of shrubbery. Decorate the shrubs with punched-out paper daisies stuck down with PVA glue and paint a spot of colour in their centres with yellow 3-D paint. Cut out a door and stick it down centrally with double-sided tape on the front of the house then stick a small gem on the door for the door knob.

6. Cut out two window frames from brown Funky Foam. Cut out two squares of blue sugar paper the same size as the frames and four curtains using scraps of paper. Stick the curtains to the side edges of the blue squares and stick these on the back of the frames. Attach the curtained windows to the front of the house with PVA glue. Two butterflies sit on the front of the house; these are punched out from coloured sugar paper and attached with a spot of PVA glue. Finally, use narrow double-sided tape and PVA glue to stick your house together, remembering to slot in the vertical supporting wall.

Mini project: Doll's house furniture

Fill your doll's house with pretty, colourful furniture! These little table and chairs are made from Hama Midi Beads which are placed one by one on a pegboard and then ironed until they are fused together. Have a good look at the construction of a table or chair in your home before designing one. Get an adult to iron the shapes once they are in place. When the beads are fused together, let them cool then turn the pegboard over and the shapes should drop off. Use a suitable glue to construct your piece of furniture.

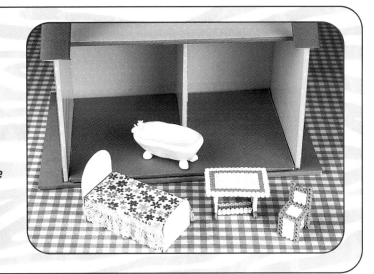

Templates

all templates are actual size

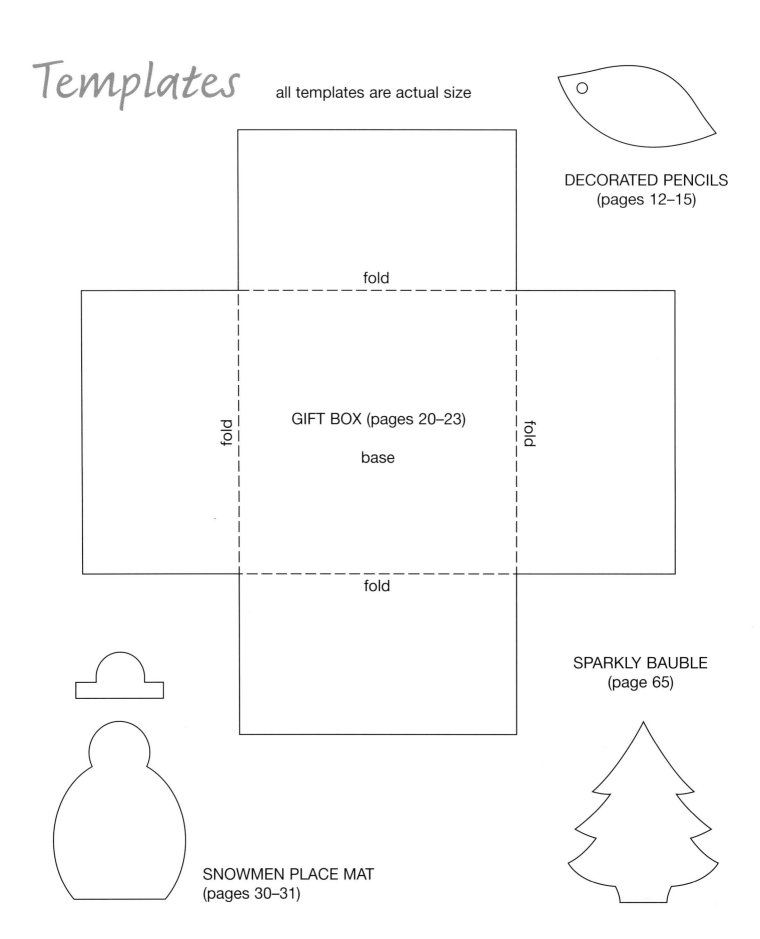

DECORATED PENCILS
(pages 12–15)

fold

fold

GIFT BOX (pages 20–23)

base

fold

fold

SPARKLY BAUBLE
(page 65)

SNOWMEN PLACE MAT
(pages 30–31)

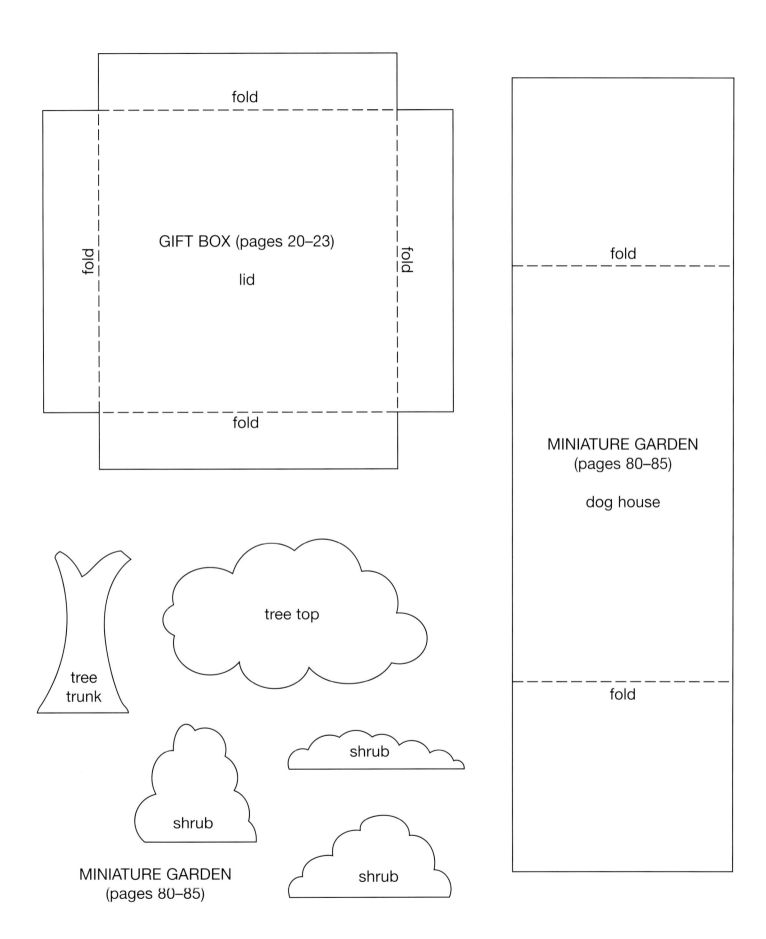

fold

fold

fold

GIFT BOX (pages 20–23)

lid

fold

fold

MINIATURE GARDEN
(pages 80–85)

dog house

fold

tree top

tree
trunk

shrub

shrub

shrub

MINIATURE GARDEN
(pages 80–85)

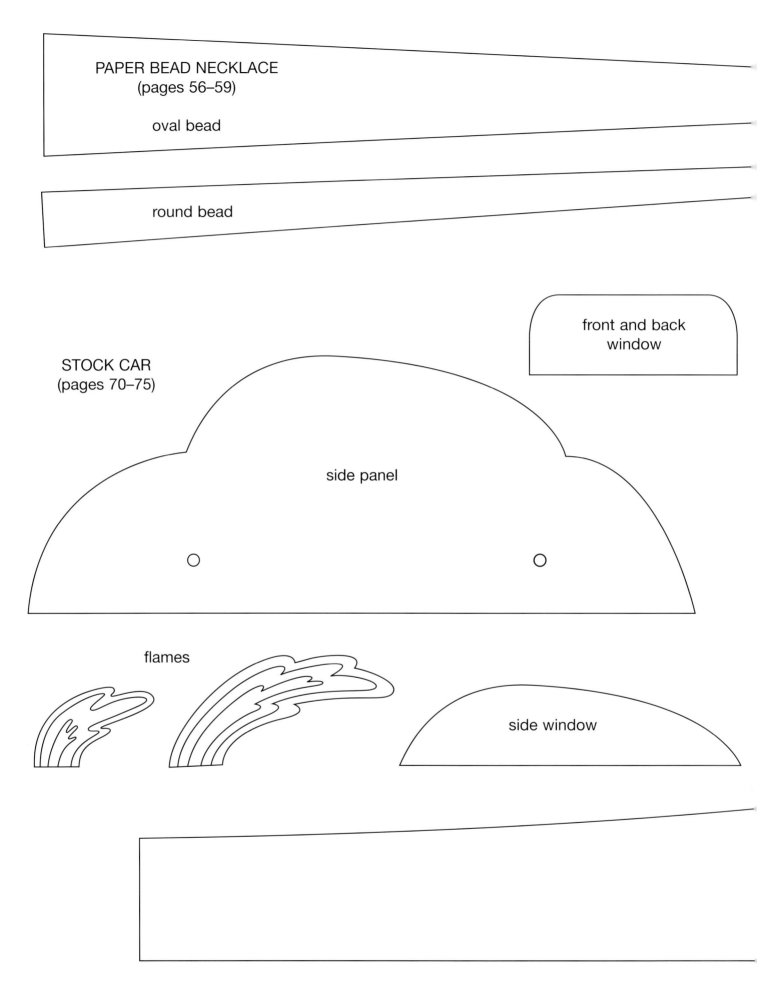

PAPER BEAD NECKLACE
(pages 56–59)

oval bead

round bead

STOCK CAR
(pages 70–75)

front and back
window

side panel

flames

side window

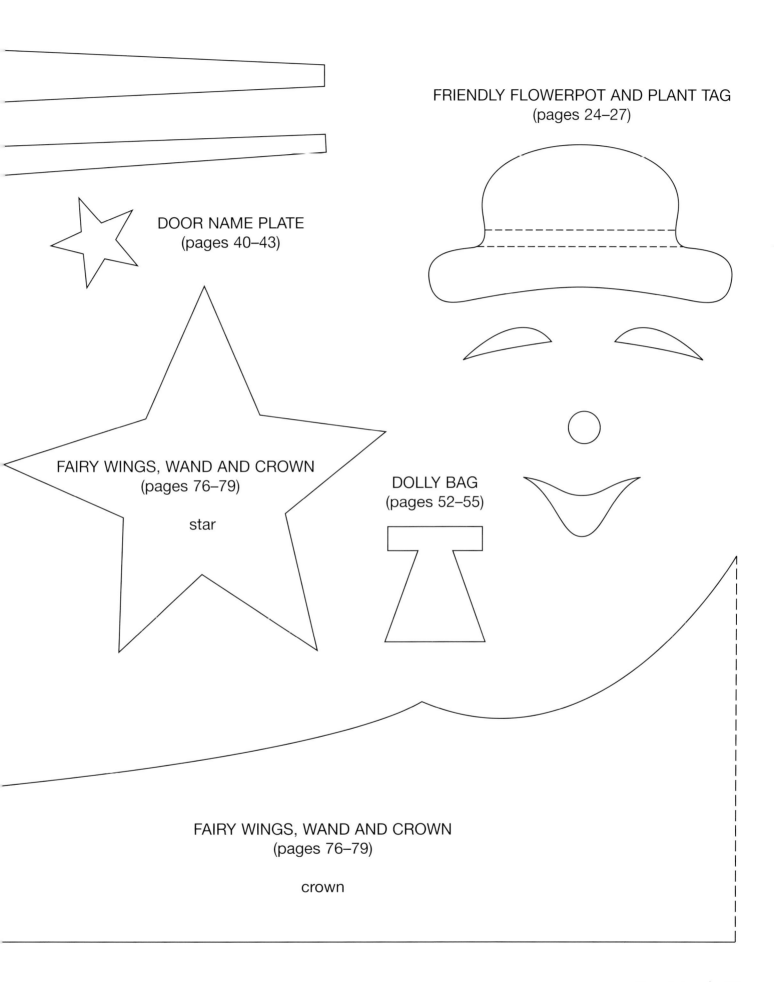

FRIENDLY FLOWERPOT AND PLANT TAG
(pages 24–27)

DOOR NAME PLATE
(pages 40–43)

FAIRY WINGS, WAND AND CROWN
(pages 76–79)

star

DOLLY BAG
(pages 52–55)

FAIRY WINGS, WAND AND CROWN
(pages 76–79)

crown

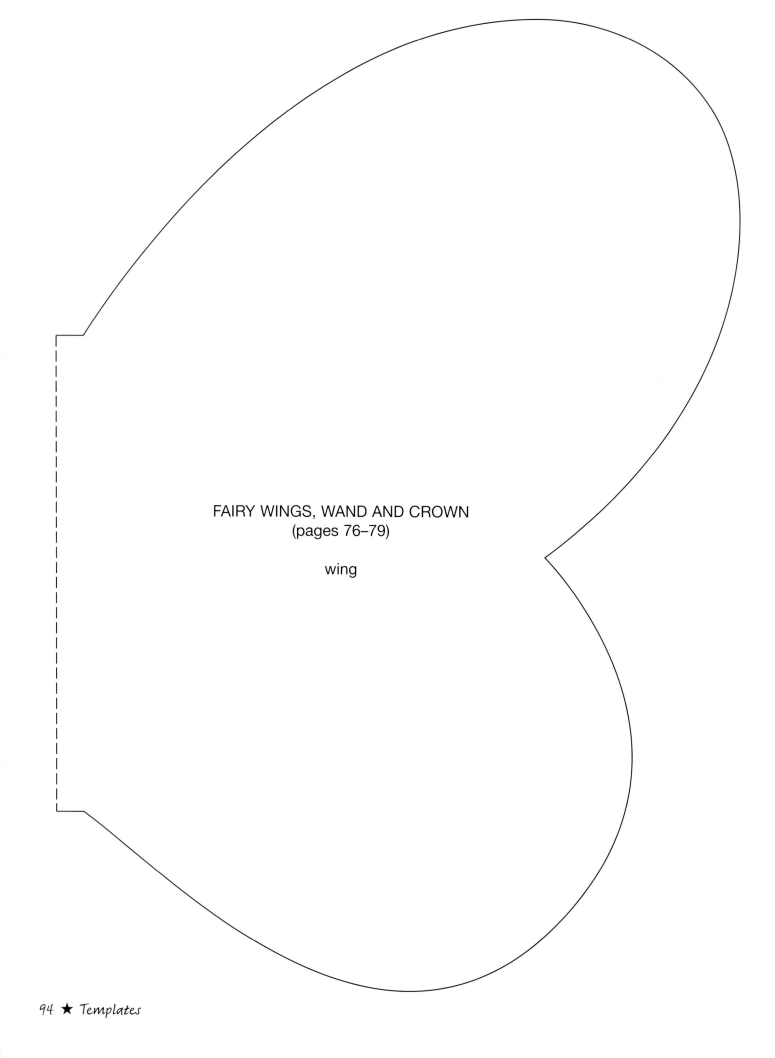

FAIRY WINGS, WAND AND CROWN
(pages 76–79)

wing

SPACE-AGE MOBILE
(pages 66–69)

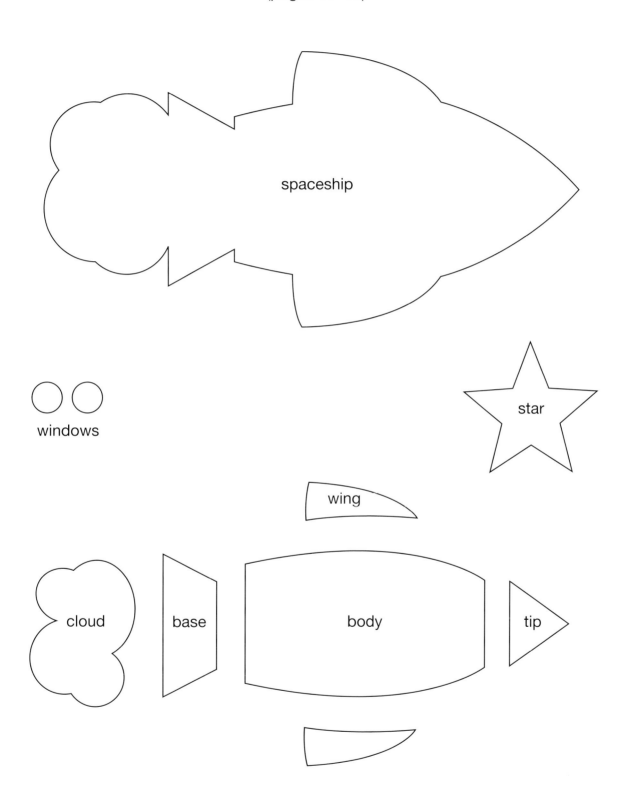

spaceship

windows

star

wing

cloud

base

body

tip

Index